Whippets
are life

Copyright © 2020 Purple Parrot Publishing

The right of Purple Parot Publishing to be identified as the author and designer has been asserted in accordance with the Copyright, Designs and Patents Act 1988.

All rights reserved. No part of this publication may be reproduced, stored in a retrieval system, or transmitted, in any form or by any means (electronic, mechanical, photocopying, recording or otherwise), without the prior written permission of the publisher.

Published by Purple Parrot Publishing

Printed in the United Kingdom

First Printing, 2020

ISBN: Print: 978-1-912677-71-9

Purple Parrot Publishing

www.purpleparrotpublishing.co.uk

Cover photographs Denise Pitcher, Amphoras Whippets, Copyright © 2020

Purple Parrot
Publishing

www.ingramcontent.com/pod-product-compliance
Lightning Source LLC
Chambersburg PA
CBHW071631080526
44588CB00010B/1362